Welcome to Iraq

By Kathryn Stevens

The Child's World®

Published by The Child's World®
1980 Lookout Drive
Mankato, MN 56003-1705
800-599-READ
www.childsworld.com

Content Adviser: Professor Paul Sprachman, Vice Director,
Center for Middle Eastern Studies, Rutgers, The State University
of New Jersey, New Brunswick, NJ
Design and Production: The Creative Spark, San Juan Capistrano, CA
Editorial: Emily J. Dolbear, Brookline, MA
Photo Research: Deborah Goodsite, Califon, NJ

Cover and title page: Kazuhiro Nogi/AFP/Getty Images
Interior photos: Alamy: 3, 8 (Linda Kennedy), 11 (The Print Collector); The Art Archive: 10 (British
Museum/Dagli Orti); Corbis: 6 (David Butow/SABA), 7 (Shepard Sherbell/SABA), 3, 9 (Namir Noor-
Eldeen/Pool/epa), 12 (Peter Turnley), 3, 19 (Kim Komenich/San Francisco Chronicle); Getty Images: 13
(Chris Hondros/AFP), 14 (Ahmad Al-Rubaye/AFP), 16 (Scott Peterson), 21 (Wathiq Khuzaie), 23 (Qassem
Zein/AFP); iStockphoto.com: 28 (Ufuk Zivana), 29 (Bryan Myhr); Landov: 20 (Atef Hassan/Reuters), 24
(Faleh Kheiber/Reuters), 25 (Ali Abbas/Pool/Reuters), 27 (Atef Hassan/Reuters); Mira.com: 30 (Sheila
McKinnon); NASA Earth Observatory: 4 (Reto Stockli); Oxford Scientific: 17 (Ann Eriksson/Nordicphotos);
Panos Pictures: 15 (Frits Meyst); SuperStock: 31 (age fotostock).
Map: XNR Productions: 5

Library of Congress Cataloging-in-Publication Data
Stevens, Kathryn, 1954–
  Welcome to Iraq / by Kathryn Stevens.
      p. cm. — (Welcome to the world)
  Includes index.
  ISBN-13: 978-1-59296-916-6 (library bound : alk. paper)
  ISBN-10: 1-59296-916-X (library bound : alk. paper)
  1. Iraq—Juvenile literature. I. Title.

DS70.62.S74 2007
956.7—dc22
                                        2007005557

Contents

Where Is Iraq?

If you looked at Earth from high above, what would you see? You would see huge land areas surrounded by water. These land areas are called continents. Iraq lies at the southwestern edge of Asia, the largest continent.

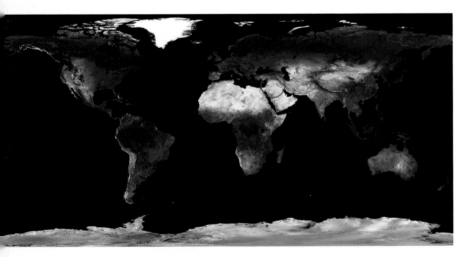

This picture gives us a flat look at Earth. Iraq is inside the red circle.

Did you **know?**

Iraq is surrounded by several other countries. They are Iran, Turkey, Syria, Jordan, Saudi Arabia, and tiny Kuwait. These countries are part of a region called the Middle East.

4

The Land

Most of Iraq is hot and dry. Some areas get only a few inches of rain each year. Few people live in the dry, rocky desert of western Iraq. The northern hills, mountains, and valleys are not as dry. Iraq's two large rivers are the Tigris (TIE-gris) and Euphrates (yoo-FRAY-tees). They flow through central Iraq

A boy tends his flock of sheep in northern Iraq.

A waterway in southern Iraq near the Persian Gulf

toward the Persian Gulf. The rivers supply much needed water for drinking and farming. Near the Persian Gulf is an area of large marshes.

Some parts of Iraq have huge underground oil fields. Many people around the world need the Middle East's oil. They use it to make fuels such as gasoline. They also use it to make plastics and countless other products.

Did you know?

Even a dry country like Iraq can have problems with too much water. Heavy rains can cause sudden, dangerous floods called **flash floods.** Flash floods in Iraq have killed people, damaged mud buildings, destroyed crops, and washed out roads.

Plants and Animals

A marbled duck in an Iraqi marsh

Most of Iraq is too hot and dry for much more than grasses and shrubs to grow. Willow and poplar trees survive in some valleys. One of Iraq's most valuable plants is the date palm. Date palms produce sweet, tasty dates that Iraqis eat or sell to other countries. Farmers grow wheat and barley crops, which they water by pumping river water onto the dry fields.

Iraq has much less wildlife than it did long ago. A few small, horned antelopes called gazelles still run free. So do some wild pigs, foxes, wolves, and hyenas. Lizards and snakes creep along the ground even in the dry deserts. Storks, hawks, and vultures soar across the sky. Ducks and geese live in the marshes.

Date palms grow next to the Euphrates River in Iraq.

In this stone carving, Assyrian farmers grow crops on a riverbank.

Long Ago

Since ancient times central and southern Iraq has been called *Mesopotamia,* or "the land between the rivers." Mesopotamia's people were some of the first farmers in the world. About 10,000 years ago, they tamed, or **domesticated,** wheat and barley and grew them for food. They domesticated animals, too, for their meat, milk, and hides. These animals included goats, sheep, pigs, donkeys, cattle, and horses.

Slowly, Mesopotamia's people changed their way of life. They stopped roaming around to hunt and stayed in one place. Villages grew into cities and then into larger kingdoms. Iraq's Sumerian, Assyrian, and Babylonian kingdoms were each very important in shaping world history.

Did you know?

Iraq's Sumerian community gave us many important inventions, including its system of writing (right), uses for the wheel, and an early calendar!

Iraqi children celebrate the fall of Basra to the British military in 2003.

Iraq Today

Many kings and emperors have ruled Iraq. In 1958, military leaders overthrew the king and created a new government. The new leaders often plotted against each other. One of them, Saddam Hussein (sah-DAHM hoo-SANE), became president in 1979. During his rule, he arrested and even killed people who opposed him.

12

Times have been very difficult for Iraq since 1979. An eight-year war with Iran that ended in 1988 killed hundreds of thousands of people. In 1990, Iraq took over a neighboring country, Kuwait. The United States, Saudi Arabia, and other nations took back Kuwait in a short but intense war called the Gulf War.

Then in 2003, American-led armed forces defeated Hussein's government. U.S., British, and other troops stayed to help maintain order and rebuild the country. Iraqis voted in their first free elections in 2005. Today the situation in Iraq is full of conflict, violence, and uncertainty. Thousands of Iraqis and U.S. soldiers have died in what is called the Iraq War.

The People

Most Iraqis are Arabs. They are also **Muslims,** or followers of the Islamic religion. Iraq has two groups of Muslims—the Shiites (SHEE-ites) and the Sunnis (SOON-eez). Shiites and Sunnis differ in some of their beliefs. Calls to prayer come

Shiites in Baghdad take part in a noontime prayer.

from **mosques,** the Islamic places of prayer, five times a day. Many of Iraq's Muslims stop whatever they are doing and pray to God, or **Allah.**

Kurds read the latest news before the start of the Iraq War in 2003.

About one-fifth of Iraq's people are Kurds rather than Arabs. Iraq's Kurds live in northeastern Iraq. The Kurds are Sunni Muslims, but they have their own culture and language. For many years they have wanted their own country, too. Saddam Hussein defeated the Kurds' attempts to become independent. He even used poison gas against them. Most Kurds supported the war against Saddam Hussein.

15

To help support his family, a young Iraqi sells soft drinks in a Baghdad street.

City Life and Country Life

Most Iraqis live in cities. Some city neighborhoods have old buildings, while others have modern high-rises. Still other

16

neighborhoods have narrow old streets and open-air markets called souks. Iraq has always bought some of its food from other countries. Many cities, especially Baghdad, were badly damaged during the Gulf War and then the Iraq

Kurdish women pick cucumbers in the fields.

War. Since the wars, much of the food and electrical supply has been cut off, and many city dwellers have had little to eat.

Life in the Iraqi countryside has never been easy. Farming in this hot, dry land is difficult. Even so, farmers continue to work hard. Most Iraqi farmers live in villages. Many live in buildings made of sun-dried mud. In marsh areas, some people travel by boat and live in houses made from reeds.

Schools and Language

Iraqi boys and girls attend primary school from age six through age eleven. There they learn reading, writing, and other basic skills. They also learn about their religion. Many students go on to secondary school for three years, where they study more math and science. Another three years of secondary school prepares some students for a training school or university.

Most of Iraq's people speak the country's official language, Arabic. Iraqi Arabic is one of many types of Arabic. Such different kinds of a language are called **dialects.** Unlike English, Arabic is read from right to left. Written Arabic uses 29 letters to represent sounds. Iraq's Kurds speak their own Kurdish language.

Did you know?

The word *Iraq* means "cliff" in Arabic.

A student recites a lesson for her teacher in Tikrit.

The oil industry is one of
Iraq's largest businesses.

Work

A worker weaves a carpet at a Baghdad factory.

Iraqis work in many types of jobs. Some still work in the oil industry, despite damage from the recent fighting. Many others raise crops and herds of animals. Some people near rivers and marshes harvest fish. During Saddam Hussein's rule, the government drained many of Iraq's southern marshes. Many marsh dwellers lost their jobs or left the country.

Other Iraqis are merchants who sell goods in stores and markets. Still others work in offices or in factories that make building materials, electronic equipment, and other products. Some Iraqis are making a better living than they did when Hussein was in power. Many others struggle to find work and feed their families.

Food

The foods of Iraq are tasty and often spicy. Iraqis do not eat pork because as Muslims they consider pigs to be unclean. They prefer lamb, chicken, and fish. Lamb is often combined with vegetables to make a spicy stew. Iraqis serve rice and bread with most meals. Pita is a flat, round bread that is hollow inside.

One well-known dish is kebab, or spiced meat and vegetables grilled on a stick. Another favorite food is *masgouf.* To make this dish, the cook grills river fish on a stick and serves it with a spicy sauce. Tea is the most popular drink in Iraq. Also popular is coffee, which is made very strong, thick, and sweet. Dairy products are made from the milk of cattle, goats, camels, sheep, and even water buffalo!

An Iraqi restaurant owner prepares kebab.

Iraqi boys at a soccer camp

Pastimes

The favorite sport of the Iraqi people is soccer. Horse racing, boxing, volleyball, weightlifting, and basketball are also popular. Iraqis take pleasure in less physical games, too, such as chess and backgammon.

The arts are important in Iraq as well. People enjoy storytelling, dance, music, poetry and writing, and the theater. Many Iraqis are skilled at traditional crafts such as weaving and pottery making. Of course visiting with friends and family is always a favorite pastime.

Ballerinas perform in a Baghdad cultural event in 2006.

25

Holidays

Iraqis celebrate a number of religious and other holidays. They also celebrate many family events, especially weddings. One important religious holiday is Eid ul-Fitr. This holiday takes place at the end of the holy month called Ramadan. During the 30 days of Ramadan, Muslims go without eating, or **fast,** from sunup to sundown. After sundown they have large family dinners called Iftar (if-TAR) to break their day of fasting. The end of Ramadan is a time for feasting, visiting, and gift-giving.

Times in Iraq are hard now. Perhaps someday you will visit Iraq, meet its interesting people, and see its ancient ruins, colorful markets, and dramatic landscapes. Iraq is truly a fascinating country with a long, proud history.

An Iraqi family shares a meal at dawn during the holy month of Ramadan.

Fast Facts About Iraq

Area: 168,754 square miles (437,072 square kilometers)—a little larger than California

Population: About 26 million people

Capital City: Baghdad

Other Important Cities: Basra, Mosul, Kirkuk, and Irbil

Money: The new Iraqi dinar (dih-NAR). One new Iraqi dinar equals 1,000 fils.

National Languages: Arabic and Kurdish (used officially in Kurdish regions). Assyrian and Armenian are also spoken in Iraq.

National Holiday: Revolution Day was celebrated on July 17 during Saddam Hussein's rule. The new Iraqi government has not yet declared a new national holiday.

Head of Government: The prime minister of Iraq

Head of State: The president of Iraq

National Flag: A flag with a red stripe across the top, a white stripe across the middle, and a black stripe across the bottom. The white stripe has three green stars and the Arabic words *Allahu Akbar* (ALL-lah ak-BAR), or "God Is Great."

Famous People:

Kadim Al Sahir: best-selling singer-songwriter

Zaha Hadid: first woman to win the Pritzker Prize for Architecture in 2004

Al'aa Hikmet: Olympic sprinter

Saddam Hussein: president of Iraq from 1979 to 2003

Dr. Iman Sabeeh: former track champion

Saladin: 12th-century Muslim hero and Kurdish leader of Egypt, Syria, Yemen, and Palestine

National Song: "My Homeland" (or *"Mawtini"*). Palestinian poet Ibrahim Touqan wrote the words to this song, which was adopted in 2004.

My homeland
My homeland
Glory and beauty
Sublimity and prettiness
Are in your hills
Life and deliverance
Pleasure and hope
Are in your atmosphere
Will I see you?
Safe and comfortable
Sound and honored
Will I see you?
In your eminence
Reaching the stars
My homeland
My homeland

The youth will not get tired
Their goal is your
   independence
Or they die
We will drink from death
But we will not be slaves to
   our enemies
We do not want
An eternal humiliation
Nor a miserable life
We do not want
But we will return
Our great glory
My homeland
My homeland

The sword and the pen
Are our symbols
Not talking nor quarreling
Our glory and covenant
And a duty to fulfill it
Shake us
Our honor
Is an honorable cause
A raised flag
O, your beauty
In your eminence
Victorious over your
   enemies
My homeland
My homeland

Iraqi Recipe*:

This recipe is for a traditional Iraqi soup made with lentils.

1 cup dried lentils
6 cups water
1 large onion, chopped

½ stick butter
½ tablespoon curry powder
½ tablespoon cumin

½ teaspoon salt

Ingredients
Put washed lentils and the water in a pot. Boil for 40 minutes with the pot half-covered. In a saucepan, sauté onion in butter and add curry powder, cumin, and salt. When tender, add to the soup and mix well. Simmer on slow heat for 10 minutes. Sprinkle cumin on top to serve.

Always ask an adult for help when cooking.

ENGLISH	HOW TO SAY IT
hello	ah sah-LAHM ah-ah-LAY-koom
good-bye	mah ahs-sah-LEH-mah
please	min FAD-lak *(to a man)* min FAD-lik *(to a woman)*
thank you	SHU-krahn
one	wah-HID
two	ith-NEEN
three	tah-LAH-tha
yes	NAAM
no	LAH

Glossary

Allah (ALL-lah) Allah is the Arabic name for God in the Islamic religion. Many of Iraq's Muslims pray to Allah five times a day.

dialects (DIE-uh-lekts) Dialects are local variations of a spoken language. Like English, Arabic has many different dialects.

domesticated (doh-MESS-tih-kay-ted) After living in the wild, people tamed, or domesticated, plants and animals. The people of ancient Mesopotamia domesticated many important food crops and animals.

fast (FAST) To fast is to go without eating. During the holy month called Ramadan, Muslims fast every day from sunup to sundown.

flash floods (FLASH FLUDZ) Flash floods are dangerous floods that happen very quickly, usually after a heavy rainfall. Flash floods have caused destruction and death in Iraq.

mosques (MOSKS) Mosques are Islamic places of prayer. Many mosques are beautiful buildings with towers, rounded domes, and colorful decorations.

Muslims (MUHS-lihms) Followers of the Islamic religion are called Muslims. Most Iraqis are Muslims.

Further Information

Read It

Corzine, Phyllis. *Modern Nations of the World—Iraq.* San Diego: Lucent Books, 2003.

Henderson, Kathy. *Lugalbanda: The Boy Who Got Caught Up in a War: An Epic Tale from Ancient Iraq.* Cambridge, MA: Candlewick Press, 2006.

King, John. *Iraq Then and Now.* Chicago: Raintree, 2006.

Samuel, Charlie. *National Geographic Countries of the World: Iraq.* New York: National Geographic Children's Books, 2007.

Look It Up

Visit our Web page for lots of links about Iraq:
http://www.childsworld.com/links

Note to Parents, Teachers, and Librarians: We routinely verify our Web links to make sure they are safe, active sites—so encourage your readers to check them out!

Index